Red for Dan

Sheila K. McCullagh

Illustrated by Pat Cook

Nelson

Tim went slowly upstairs. Aunt May was still out, and there was no light in Miss Miff's room. Even Mr. Bunce was out. The house was empty.

He left the lights on in the hall and on the landing. He knew that Aunt May would be cross, and say that he was wasting money, but the house seemed so dark and empty that he wanted light.

Tim went into his own room, and shut the door. He wished he had a wooden bar to put across it. He pulled the table across the door, and put the chair against the table.

Tim went over to the window, and looked out. Over the dark roofs, the clouds were black and heavy with rain. He heard thunder rumbling in the distance.

He shut the catch on the window.

He was just turning back into the room, when he saw a light swinging round and round in a circle in Arun's window.

He slipped across and switched out the light, picked up his torch, and ran back to the window. He swung his torch round and round in a circle.

There were two short flashes.

Tim remembered what that meant. It meant: "Are you all right?"

He sent one white flash back.

Arun's torch swung round in a green circle.

Tim changed to green, and made a circle in reply.

Arun's light went out.

Tim switched the light in his room on again. He put his torch down on the table by his bed.

He felt very much better.

He left the light on, and got into bed. He was going to have all the lights on, whatever Aunt May said.

He lay listening, and watching the door. But nothing happened, and at last he fell asleep.

Tim must have been asleep for a long time, when there was a loud crash of thunder overhead.

He sat up in bed.

The light was out. The room was in darkness.

There was a flash of lightning, followed by another roll of thunder.

Then the rain came.

Tim could hear it beating against the window, as if there were people outside trying to get in.

He felt for his torch, and flashed it on.

Tim found the matches, and lit the candle by his bed. He switched off the torch. He always liked candle-light. It looked so yellow and warm.

He got out of bed, and went over to the window. It was very dark outside. All the lights were out in houses round The Yard. The street lamp was out, too. The rain was beating down, and he could hear the wind moaning.

Another flash of lightning lit The Yard. Tim stared down.

A dark figure was standing down there in the rain. He had a long, black cloak and a three-cornered hat. He was looking up towards Tim's window. Tim saw that he had a black mask across his eyes.

Then everything was dark again, as the thunder rolled overhead.

Tim slipped back into bed. He sat up with his arms round his knees, listening. He felt as if he was waiting for something, but he didn't know what he was waiting for.

The wind dropped.
The rain stopped.
Everything was very still.

The stairs creaked outside the door.
Tim listened. Was there someone in the house? He held his breath.
Then he heard a pattering and scratching in the wall.
"It's just a mouse," Tim said aloud. "It's just a mouse in the wall."
But he wasn't sure.
There was a sudden tapping at the window.
Tim gripped his knees with his arms.
Tap! Tap, tap, tap!
He got out of bed and went to the window.

A big crow was standing on the sill, tapping the glass. As soon as it saw Tim, it lifted its wings, flopped off the sill, and flew away into the dark.

Was it a crow?

What was it?

Tim felt his hair lifting.

It was very dark, down there in The Yard. The darkness seemed to be still thicker under the big tree. There was something moving there.

Tim stared down. Was that a horse? It looked like a horse and rider, down there in the shadows.

As he stared out into the dark, Tim saw a sudden circle of light in Arun's window.

He slipped back for his torch, ran to the window, and swung it round in an answering circle.

At once, there was one long and one short flash. Tim knew what that meant. Arun was coming over.

Then there was one red flash.

Red for danger!

Tim slipped the top of the torch to red, and sent three red flashes across the dark Yard.

Arun's window went dark. Arun must be on his way. He couldn't let Arun come along that back lane alone. The Hidden People might be there. They might even be in the house.

Tim pulled on his clothes as fast as he could. He lifted the wooden chair back, and pulled the table away from the door.

He switched on his torch, and slipped downstairs.

There was no one on the landing.

Tim could hear Mr. Bunce snoring, as he crept past his door. Tim had never thought that he would be glad to hear Mr. Bunce's snores, but he was.

He unbolted the back door as silently as he could, and slipped out.

He flashed the light quickly round the back yard, but it was empty. He ran over to the back gate, and out into the lane.

That was empty, too. Then a torch shone at the corner.

"Arun?" Tim called softly.

"Hallo, Tim," Arun's voice called back.

In another minute, Arun was with him, and they were safely in the back yard.

As Tim shut the gate and bolted it, he felt something against his leg, and jumped back.

"What's that?" he whispered.

"It's only Sebastian," said Arun softly. "I found him outside the back door, when I came out of the house. He came with me. Let him in. He's very wet."

"Why did you flash red?" whispered Tim, as he opened the back door.

"I looked out, and there was a dark shadow at your window. I knew you must have a candle alight, and there was something trying to get in."

"It was a crow," said Tim. "But the Hidden People are in The Yard. I saw them. Come in."

Tim locked the back door carefully, and led the way upstairs.

It was only when they went into his own room, that he saw that Arun was carrying a long bit of wood.

"What's that for?" he asked.

"It's a bar for the door," said Arun.

Arun pulled two big handles, some screws and a screwdriver out of one of his pockets. As Tim and Sebastian watched, he screwed two handles on to the door posts, one on each side. Then he pushed the bar of wood across the door, through the handles.

"That will hold the door," he said. "Now for the light switch."

Arun took some cup-hooks out of his pocket. He screwed them in along the skirting board all round two sides of the room. The first one was just under the light switch, and the last one under the head of Tim's bed.

He pulled out a ball of thin string. He pushed up the light switch, and tied one end of the string to it. Then he ran the string under the cup-hooks. He cut it off, and tied the end to the head of Tim's bed.

"Now you won't have to get out of bed to put the light on," said Arun. "Just pull the string."

Tim pulled the string. The switch clicked down, but the light didn't come on.

"The lightning must have struck the wires again," said Arun.

"The light never works when the Hidden People are about," said Tim. "But thanks all the same. It's a good idea. I'll be glad to be able to switch the light on in the night, when I'm in bed."

There was another burst of rain against the window. The window shook, and rattled in a gust of wind.

Tim went over to it and looked out into the night.

It was then that he saw the wild witches. The clouds parted, and he saw them riding on their broomsticks high up over the roofs and across and over The Yard.

"Look!" cried Tim. "Look, Arun, look!"
Arun ran across to the window, and stared out.

"What is it?" he said. "What can you see?"

"The witches!" whispered Tim. His face was white and his hands shook. "The wild witches! Look at them, up there over the roofs!"

"It's no good, Tim," said Arun. "I can't see them. I can see the black clouds flying in the wind, but that's all."

As Tim watched, the witches swung to one side, and were gone.

He turned back into the room.

"Look at Sebastian!" he said.

Sebastian was standing on the end of the bed, watching them. His back was up and his hair was standing on end.

Arun went over and stroked him. Sebastian's hair sank down. He rubbed himself against Arun's hand.

"What we need is some more light," said Arun. "Something to eat, too."

Arun seemed to have endless pockets. He pulled some candles out of one of them, and some tin lids out of another. He set a ring of lighted candles in the tin lids on the floor.

Then he sat down on the bed, took two big slices of cake out of his pocket, and handed one to Tim.

"Let's have a midnight feast," he said. "We need one."

"When are you going back?" asked Tim, munching his cake. He broke off a bit and gave it to Sebastian, who ate it, purring.

"I'll stay till daylight," said Arun. "You get back into bed. I'll sleep on the floor."

"You can't do that," said Tim.

"You just watch me!" said Arun. "I often sleep on the floor. I like it."

Tim pulled two blankets off his bed, and gave them to Arun.

Arun blew out the candles on the floor, and lay down.

Tim lay on the bed, just as he was. The candle by his bed was still alight, and he left it burning.

Sebastian curled up on the bed at his feet.

It was bright daylight when he opened his eyes again.

Arun was standing by the bed.

"I'd better go now, Tim," he said. "They'll be wondering where I am. I can hear someone downstairs, too."

Tim jumped up.

"I'll let you out the back way," he said. "Aunt May will be in the kitchen."

They crept downstairs. There was no one in the hall.

Tim opened the back door, and Arun slipped out.

"See you later, Tim," he whispered.

"I – I have to go and see Melinda today," Tim said. "I'll be going after breakfast."

Arun turned back. "I'll come with you," he said.

Tim shook his head. "I have to go alone," he said. "Melinda wouldn't be there, if anyone came with me."

"All right," said Arun. "I'll see you when you get back. Take care of yourself, Tim."

Tim nodded.

Arun slipped across the back yard and out of the gate.

Sebastian was still curled up on his bed, fast asleep, when Tim went back into his room. He lifted the little cat on to the floor, picked up his blankets, and made the bed.

Sebastian jumped back on to it, and went to sleep again.

"Tim! Are you up yet?" Aunt May called up the stairs. "Tim! It's time for breakfast."

"Coming," called Tim.

He splashed his face with cold water, dried himself quickly, and ran downstairs to the kitchen.